A LIVING ANYTIME

for Jim
Read These poems
in maine & enjoy
War wishe
Judith Steinbergh

A Living Anytime

POEMS BY
JUDITH W. STEINBERGH

TROUBADOUR PRESS
BOSTON, MA

Cover painting:
Striped Robe, Fruit and Anemones, by Henri Matisse
Courtesy of The Baltimore Museum of Art:
The Cone Collection, formed by Dr. Claribel Cone and
Miss Etta Cone, Baltimore, Maryland
BMA 1950.263
Photograph by John Tennant

Kezar Lake Illustration:
Copyright © 1988 Robin Kroin

Cover Calligraphy:
Olga Emmel

Book design:
Barbara Wolinsky
Trillium Studios
Norwell, MA

First Edition

Library of Congress Catalog Card Number 87-051334
ISBN 0-944941-00-1

What follows is a work of imagination. The characters,
incidents, places and dialogues are products of the author's
creativity and are not to be construed as real.

For inquiries and catalog, write to:
Troubadour Press
A subsidiary of Troubadour, Inc.
ll Spring Valley Road
West Roxbury, MA 02132

FOR ROBIN

ACKNOWLEDGMENTS

Grateful acknowledgments is made to these magazines
which published: "Religion," "Give Peace a Chance," "Giving
Over Control," "Research," in *Sojourner;* "At the Lake With-
out Kids," in *Dark Horse;* "Mica," in *Harbor Review;* "Arguing
with Joyce," "Nights Under the Trumpet Vine," and "These
Days," in *Calyx;* "Silver," and "One Evening When I Was
Busy," in *Stone Country;* "Past Time," in *Tendril* and in *86/87
Anthology of Magazine Verse and Yearbook of American Poetry*
(Monitor); "Leaving," in *Sunrust;* "Blackout," "Looking for
Camp To-Ho-Ne," "A Living Anytime," in *The Worcester
Review;* "Gem," in *Texas Review, New England Sampler;*
"There Are No Rules," in *Wilory Farm Anthology,*
(Second Prize); "Womanfriend," in *Woman 3 Anthology;*
"Initiation at Bash Bish Falls," won the Word Works
"Washington Prize," 1983. This manuscript was a finalist in
the Stone Country Competition (1983), AWP (1984),
Brittingham Prize (85, 86, 87), the Word Works Competition,
and Second Runner Up in the San Jose Competition chosen
by Lucille Clifton (1986.)

ONE
Now that we're middle-aged we're reciting Wordsworth.

TWO
In those hours I'm home among the still things.

THREE
It is a question of timing.

FOUR
So much of my life crowds in on me here.

FIVE
One evening when I was busy typing, my daughter turned.

S<small>IX</small>

What if you came to the lake for two weeks and
the mountains never appeared.

S<small>EVEN</small>

Too many things dying and growing up.

INTRODUCTION

Judith Steinbergh, in her third book of poetry,
A LIVING ANYTIME, weaves and wanders, gathers and
sifts, stirs, circles, and it's all here: friends, family, love,
work, burdens, blessings, sweet stews, and a lot of laughter.
Beyond danger and the usual breakdowns, the woman is
coping not moping; and the gifts of the mundane and the
gifts of the mythological are interchangeable. Amidst the
whole-life kit and caboodle, the litanies and listings, the poet,
in the center of her age, is celebrating. Everything is in
process: bud/blossom/body. Throw chronology away, and
let it all circulate in the welcoming air, the warming soup.
The dead and the living forgive and forget, nod and begin to
dance. The foreground recedes, the background begins to
brag, the young grow up and away; the woman, well, she
keeps on weaving these poems with humor and humanness
and courage.

Let's place her. This is not the poetry of an urban guer-
rilla or a rural visionary. This is the work of a woman who
lives on a tree-lined street close to Boston in a big old house
with a porch, surrounded somewhere by children, friends, a
loving companion and sustaining demanding work. This is
Saturday and Sunday and the whole damn week ahead, lists
and learning, lust, lore, and curiosity. This is sensuosity so
sweet it hurts. This is a woman who focuses a keen observ-
ing intelligence on the natural wonders of the whirl and
world. This is the rush and roar of an overextended life and
the determination to find the precious space between, so the
words, once found, can come to fruit.

*Wait. Do not make conclusions based on what will surely
change. It is not the end of art or love. Just low tide. A twice
daily phenomenon the sea puts up with, its life seething below the
unglamorous mud. The tide will come in. Feelings will seep into
the marsh grass. And words, real ones, the ones that prickle and
swim, will lap at the doorstep again.*

It's simple: what comes in, comes in, what goes out, goes
out blessed and bearable. It's all here: the erratic, the erotic,
the quixotic. We join her for the prism of seasons and
sadness, the glint of wind and gesture: spin-offs, reflections,
light, delight. Specific. It rhymes with pacific. Both are at
work in Judith Steinbergh's A LIVING ANYTIME.

Elizabeth McKim

ONE

Now that we're middle aged, we're reciting Wordsworth.

Past Time

And now my heart with pleasure fills
And dances with the daffodils.

William Wordsworth

Now that we're middle aged, we're reciting Wordsworth
on the front porch on a Sunday afternoon finally savoring
the words like the strawberries in the colander between
us, letting the words bypass our minds and slip into our
hearts so that even the most innocent phrase catches at
our feelings like a thorn and makes us weep. It's odd
when a friend or even worse a stranger arrives and we're
on the verge of tears over a line that once bored us.

There is no explaining the impact of words. The kids are
half grown, some of our parents have died, we have lived
half our lives and in that time, enough has happened to
strip daffodils down to their truth. Perhaps we should
hide poems from the children until words take on the
power of memory or hope, until they darken like storm
clouds or glitter like the face of the sea under the moon.
Then the poems are spoken with the import of weather,
of celebration and defeat, then words swell like silk
banners far above the page and simple conversation is
as tender as a hand stroking your hair.

WILDLIFE

I live in a major city of the northeast and the wild life
that abounds during the day includes fat crows,
scurrilous jays, rodeos of squirrels, and our own
personal skunk who likes us to know he's around,
dogs, cats, an elusive raccoon, slugs, earwigs, and
carpenter ants that could take an anteater any day.
But at night in the humid dark of the street when all
else is silent, a bird sings like a diva, a multitude of
songs, pure and joyous, filling the whole neighbor-
hood as if it were a bowl with cream.
It sings from the roof of the grey victorian house.
In the day, I only see ordinary brown birds perched
on the eaves. This bird would have a startling white
ring or fuchsia plumes or wings of gauze or roses.
It would be laying over on its way to Eleuthera
or Brazil, a bird who knew Aztecs or Tutankhamen
or Pericles or Keats. What have we in the city done
to deserve this singing? Up along the coast, the
piercing cries of sea birds haunt the fishermen and in
the peace of the north Maine woods, the loons sling
their songs out like silver stones, but here where
houses usurp the grass and we can count the signifi-
cant trees on two hands, where traffic
and trolleys and sirens and joggers and raucous
teenagers are all the wilderness we have, this bird,
this warbler, elegant and somehow as wild as any
creature, wakes us in the deepest night and holds us
as if its songs fell like golden rings around our
hearts.

SILVER

like strands in our hair veins the grasses.
Silver grass, silver bellies of the gulls in
blue silver sky, black silver beach plum bark
spouting silver white blossoms, silver flies,
silver wasps, silver wind, silver heart of the
sea thumping silvery dunes, whole schools of
silver fish flinging themselves out of their
pond flashing their scales, slapping the water
like the silver snap of neon, silver your hair
lit by sun, green silver undersides of lilac
leaves, silver capillaries of poison ivy, silvered
shingles of the weathered cottage. Everything
shines at us like a hot haze, a salt mist,
particles of silver swarm before our eyes,
bead on our lips and eyelashes, the points of
pine needles glint, bark of wild cherry shimmers.
There is no dull thing when the body is open,
the air hovers just above the ground iridescent
as dragon fly wings, silver gold hairs rise off
your shoulders like spikes on dandelion leaves,
like vines of sunspots, silver necklaces of sweat
ring your forehead, and the sun, molten silver coin
behind your head, lets out all its heat.

There Are No Rules

and my ex-husband on his fortieth birthday shows up to
pick up his sister who is visiting me and brings his girlfriend
who is still in college leaving her on my front porch to chat
about her major while he runs upstairs to shower and my
lover comes to observe my daughter's classroom with his ex-
wife who is not even his ex-wife yet while I am there visiting
and we are cordial, we are more than cordial, we are inti-
mate in this irony. You think everything is set, maybe no
one is speaking and lawyers are handling it all when the
rules change: my ex-husband's second wife leaves, my ex-
husband calls for a date, my ex-husband invites my lover
and me to a hot tub party, we are all in the steam together
eating olives and drinking beer and talking about real estate
development. Who knows what to expect next. Even
Neptune switched orbits with Pluto and Mount St. Helens,
dormant for centuries, bellows fire again. The whole
planet's still settling, roads mean nothing, the formal lines of
communication, separation agreements are all fragile as
telephone wires crossing the San Andreas fault, custody like
the mid-oceanic rift releases enough heat to warm a popula-
tion. We build houses as if we were immune, we count on
the continents, we ignore their drift. Beneath us a cauldron
boils daily and doesn't make the news. Stable is a word
we've invented so we can sleep.

LUCKILY A GORGEOUS OCTOBER DAY

when the rocket was brought out, slim and silver,
finned and winged, by no less than ten children,
five adults, and two dogs, all of whom huddled and
jumped back no less than sixteen times, counting
down to blastoff over and over, each time the shout
meeting only stillness, the parents crouched now,
smoking and checking directions over the tiny
tower like generals, the children fighting and
tripping over the dogs who were the only things
blasting off, the crimson leaves falling on cue,
the father who had so carefully supervised, shall
we say, the building of this object about to show
his son now where power lay, was smiling tensely.
Everything was as it should be. Thus, when it left
the ground with a hiss sliding into the blue
October sky, we were too surprised to cheer for a
moment, our mouths were wide, until the rocket
hesitated at its invisible peak, tipped, and out
bloomed its tiny parachute with no less than ten
children chasing it across the field. I would have been
as happy to have it stay on earth, a symbol for how we build,
not really expecting to leave the ground,
unlike the kids who know whatever they want, they'll get,
whatever their parents touch, will fly.

Playground Clean-up

It is Saturday morning and somehow the children and I have
dragged ourselves and our brooms to the school playground
where we, along with other devoted families, have vowed
we will clean up all the broken glass. The children are
pecking in the grass like hens, following cracks to the far
corners of the asphalt yard, trying to fill their bags to win
the prize: five dollars worth of treasures from the school
store for the child who gathers the most. They are guarding
their little mounds of glass. I, too, am crouched down on the
ground picking up shards of Pepsi and beer bottles as if this
were as valuable as a dig in Israel, as if this jagged rubbish
held secrets we were dying to know and in a way it does.
It tells me I will murder the next teenager who absent-
mindedly drops his bottle of Sprite by the side of the courts
whereas last week, I didn't care, it tells me that here
at middle age, I am doing what city parents for centuries
have been doing on Saturday mornings in spring, gathering
broken glass like wildflowers, that I am actually happy
there is broken glass to gather. It brings us together like an
ancient tribe, our down vests and brooms, our worn jeans
left over from the sixties, assuring us we are growing old
with shared battles, though now our cause, and blistered
palms keep our children from throwing baseballs full of
shrapnel, from puncturing tires of their ten speed bikes.
It tells me the smashed gum wrappers and cigarette butts,
the ordinary refuse of our lives is worth little. It is the
broken glass that wins the prize, glittering, dangerous,
filling our children's dreams with stickers and rabbits' feet,
reminding us, the dutiful parents, of the hard edge,
the hurting edge of what holds light.

WAITING IN LINE AT THE POST OFFICE

Just knowing the clerks are rambling hazily through
the shelves of packages which are filed in an order
that ensures they will never be found, just watching
them leaf through the drawers of stamps for a rare
8¢ number that's been out of print for years, just
hearing them stop service altogether to chat with the next
clerk about last week's wedding, it's no wonder the sign says:
ASSAULT ON A POSTAL WORKER IS A FEDERAL OF-
FENSE. I say to myself, they're humans, they deserve to talk,
but the line has snaked into the lobby and out the doors and
will soon cross the trolley tracks, and furthermore,
the line has not inched forward for what seems like months.
We are like the oversized tail of a dinosaur, tyrannosaurus -
post office. It should be extinct, but it lurks, huge and small-
brained eating its victims in its own way, and should we even
reach the window, a goal as inaccessible as the crest of Mt.
Everest, it will be for stamps which have shrunk so small
one needs tweezers to hold them, bifocals to see them and
Elmer's to stick them. Better to take the letter yourself, come
face to face with your mother-in-law or your daughter who's
defected to Egypt or the manager of Mobil who awaits your
check with an eagerness unimaginable, better to give it up,
these feeble symbols of communication, and let the granite
edifice crumble into dust.

CLIMBING BALDFACE

Out in the open at last after two hours of climbing.
"Very steep," the guide book warns. It doesn't say
you have to climb it on your belly. Stand straight
and your back is horizontal to the valley, far, too
far below. Yee gads, slither up the long granite
rivers and drag your legs up ledges higher than
your breast. "Spiderwoman's coming!" I holler to
my partner who is much too terrified to look back.
"What a great view!" he calls, focusing on the blue-
berry bushes pushing up through every crack, black
with luscious berries. My heart is so loud in my
ears, I can't think a thought, my breath reminds me
of a hurricane. What a woman! Thirty-eight. Mother
of two. Conquering fear, finding the next hand-hold.
I'm sweating from pores I never knew I had. The grade
gentles, only a false top, it turns out, but enough to
save my life. Someone's grandma, in blue polyester
pants, an apron, I swear, and a straw bonnet, is smiling
at her granddaughter and patting her fat bags of blue-
berries. She is as fresh as if she'd stepped into her
garden to pick a daisy, as if a helicopter had dropped
her off at the peak, or an elevator only she knew of
zoomed through the dark mountain's core to the richest
blueberry fields in the state, as if she weren't heading down
the steep granite face we'd just scaled up,
 neither of her hands free for clutching.
"Nice day for picking berries, dearie" she must have
warbled to her granddaughter, neglecting to mention
the climb. "Nice harvest," I nod, trying to smile
through my panting. Grannie, I want to be like you.
Yankee, yankee, yankee. Blue and blue.

PICKING BLUEBERRIES ON BALDFACE

We're at the peak now, nearly four thousand feet up,
the whole summit bald as Buddha, save for a thin veneer
of blue fruit. While I pick them, the berries actually
grow bigger absorbing sun, as I do naked to the waist.
While I pick them, my thumb actually gets softer and
the thick clusters of globes fall into my palm. I
harvest from each patch, small deep blues, fuller
silver-frosted blues, and the almost black patent ones.
I want to taste each subtle flavor of sun. The berries
lead me on, across the south face, under the ledges.
I sit in each scratchy patch, I lie in them, putting
handfuls of samples into my mouth, my pants stained
with purple. This will be no ordinary pie, it will have
four hawks gliding over it and views of the whole
Presidential Range and across Maine to the sea. This
pie will have bitter winters of ice and wind so fierce
the ears sting, white blossoms that covered the cheeks
of the mountain with new fuzz, and a deep still drinking
of sun. And the jam will have kept, along with a bit of
pale lichen, a whole peak from eroding. Where nothing
grew but the slow circles of lichen, the blue fruit
hung on. Tenacious and sweet. Eat then. Valleys and
villages, weather and stars. These berries nudged clouds.

WHAT A GARDEN!

This is my time: summer skies, a breeze flaps
my papers, my desk overlooks the leaves and blooms
of the rose of Sharon. My time to fool with the piano,
its cool ivory keys, trying what I don't know how to do,
fingering melodies, leaping across linoleum floors,
dreaming of the living who come up silver in water,
thinking of the dead still living, flowing over,
falling out of my mind onto the page, making new
bouquets of words, fleshy roses, wild tiger lilies,
blue, blue lupine, my aunt crazy and sweet as honey-
suckle, my mother fierce as the striped bees, my
grandma's voice as breathy as the black wind
in the leaves at night, the invisible wind, singing
into mockingbird courting, into dragonfly flight.
Summer, and it's my time with friends, with fruits
of mango and backyard raspberries, with fragrant souls
and tenacious spirits of those I've loved. What a garden!
Tomatoes, and the tangy stories of our deceased.
God blessed me and gave me this salad, this family,
this fertile plot where everything roots and grows.

Two

In those hours I'm home among the still things.

Letting the Parakeet Fly

In those hours I'm home among the still things,
paintings, plants, piles of clean laundry, drafts
of unfinished poems, I let the parakeet out of
his cage, free in the house, if one considers
that free. I do it, I think, to relieve the guilt
that comes from owning a caged bird in the first
place. Also I like the pale blue blurs it makes
crossing the room, crepe paper streamers or silk.
When it flaps its short take-offs and shorter
landings, a wind fills the room, a sound like
torches or locusts. While I work, I know that
among the quiet, something moves, breathes, makes
heat, weather, whole flocks of geese. Something
becomes more than it is, stirs up the mind,
the air. Sets my own words free.

MICA

When we stumbled on the abandoned mine
it was far better than coming on silver or gold.
Mica, glittering like small mirrors
sewn into cloth from India or stacked
in thick decks protruding from the cliffs,
or strewn among the lumps of littered quartz,
iridescent as fish. We took as much
as we could carry down the mountain
and spread now on the kitchen table
is a vast treasure of shine. We sit
over coffee catching up with friends.
What new events have pressed our old
strata down. We peel layers away
absentmindedly. Imagine a rock that bends,
that slides away from itself, that's
transparent as glass. The mica
takes up half the table, but we
do not pack it away. It is one thing
changing into another: flakes of moonlight
into scales upon the lake we have just left,
summer silver into the brittleness of fall.
This is a time of transition. We may
actually stabilize, become dull. But all
winter the mica will gleam, becoming,
possibly, the first snowfall.

APRIL SUNDAY

April Sunday on my porch swing
pathetic though it is holding us up
with glue and staples, now loge seats
overlooking the children gradually moving
the contents of the house onto the porch,
down the concrete steps like a glacier,
seeping along the sidewalk and onto
the street, insistent and irreversible:
mattresses, electric blankets, all the
animals, stuffed and otherwise, high
chairs, food, real and questionable, bikes,
tricycles, big wheels, tire pumps, wrenches
necessary for their repair, training wheels,
all purpose oil, suntan oil, umbrellas,
champagne glasses, all the sections of the
Globe, lemonade stands, book stalls, roller
skates, an instant market place in Bombay
with fresh flies and wasps promising nests
right here on Evans Road.

We swing a little in the warm sun
and get nothing read
and get no taxes done.

The children marry each other and go to sleep
and get up and go to work and eat dinner maybe
twelve or fifteen times, they put gas in their
tricycles, they listen to the heart of my car
with a stethoscope, they water the tulips
they've just stepped on with squirt guns,
they walk a tightrope on the street, do cart-
wheels on bareback, ride motorcycles through fire.

Between the red car at the Smith's and the silver one
at the Lieberman's, it all happens; and we,
who have only this to offer, witness
what is given us with grace.

Fruit Flies Swarming

as if my kitchen were the back yard of the Dole pineapple
juice factory. At night I scrub the kitchen clean and spray
them dead, a million or so heaped like a sand dune of fruit
flies. But while I sleep, the last two bugs hidden in the sugar
bowl are screwing away like mad, activity my kitchen has
never seen, nor have I, but at dawn when the kids are
clamoring for Wheaties, a thousand newborns swarm over
their heads. Fruit is unnecessary, they live on toast ends,
juice stains on the curtains, the possibility of dinner a week
from now. Every closet, every cupboard has its own popula-
tion, even the freezer has its share, frozen, yes, but waiting
for the thaw. I drink a glass of wine and four flies drown
under my lips. They pursue me into the shower, into my
office, yes, one hovers now over the typewriter, breaking up
my friendships which survived my babies, divorce, and my
mother's death, but will not bear the tedious persistence of
fruit flies. This is worse than nuclear proliferation, worse
than exponentiation, this is a pain in the ass, worse than
guerrilla warfare, the enemy surrounds us and dies gladly,
knowing the future is assured.

RESEARCH

I'm in the kitchen bagging the trash while my son complains
that I never let him watch T.V. (he's only watched six
straight hours today), and my daughter who's deep in pre-
adolescent gloom is shrieking with her best friend because
the parakeet is loose and is dive bombing my head
like the blue baron, in other words, the typical Sunday
evening scene, when the phone rings and a voice asks
would I be part of a study about parents and kids
(and parakeets? I ask), to see how parents cope with
everyday stress. I keep bagging the trash with the bird
perched and no doubt shitting on my head and the girls
howling so loudly I can barely hear the social researcher
saying that my husband gave her this number. Oh, he's not
my husband anymore, I say. Can you talk for a minute?
she asks. Sure, I say nearly shouting over the din of kids
who leap from counter to floor and over the stove to catch
the bird who has about as much interest in being caught
(and studied) as I do at this moment. But I can't let you
know right now, (even she is laughing, thank god), because
I'm in the middle of too much "everyday life and stress"
to think. Research, I reflect later as I scrape my daughter's
attempts at pizza dough from the kitchen floor, has
to be done. It's like bagging trash, or making it. Her lead
was correct. Come on over, I should have said, and give me
a hand.

GIVE PEACE A CHANCE

I had to get an operation to get some peace. I didn't actually
go so far as to invent the symptoms (although this is not out
of the question), but I went leaping into that hospital as if it
were a plane ticket to the islands, away from my kids and
cooking and cleaning and teaching and four classes a day. I
took my most important shells and stones and beads. My
nurse Bessie winked away a lot of rules like not sticking
photos on the walls and my nurse Lenora busied herself
elsewhere while my man lounged on my bed until real late
that first night. Even after the morphine and pentothal,
teams of masked bandits after my treasures, and lovely silk
stitches, I lay afloat on sunlight in my room again, at peace
for the first time in a decade, sipping ice water down a
parched throat, letting calm fill up my knuckles and knees,
my elbows, the long curved fibula and the dark explored
cavities of my body. No way I was going home. I had to
faint in the lav to convince the staff to let me stay. The
daffodils opened their mouths gently and visitors pushed
pastels like chips of sky and lips over rough paper. I was
thin and green as a leaf on a river. Oh give me peace once
in a long while.

GOSSIP

She was a mother you could count on. She was like the sun
and the moon, the seasons, the constellations, the orbit
of Saturn, the laws of gravity. She could cope. Everyone
took it for granted. She did this for years and years and
years until it was like breathing, like getting up, like blood
in the veins, and the husband came and went on the train
or the plane carrying a briefcase or a suitcase. He was a
footnote to the thesis of their lives. So when he left for the
west coast for six weeks, everything seemed as it always
seemed, but back in the suburbs, she mailed the ticket to his
mother in Wales, painted the trim, took his shirts to the
cleaner, cooked a week of meals and froze them, booked
one passage on a freighter with no return, and four days
after her mother-in-law arrived and six days before her
husband was due home, she left it all behind, ruining in one
act a reputation it took her years to create, scandalizing
a community, stirring up worse than dust, leaving hus-
bands and wives sweating in their king-sized beds.

WOMAN FRIEND

You come bounding in with your daughter and the news
that you've met a man, are planning to move in, move
out of your place two blocks from me, move to some
street you insist is in Brookline, but which I know is in
Cambridge, and I look at Jamie who is crying over
having to change schools, and since I'm sure I'll never see
either of you again, I cry too. We drive to my husband's
editor's apartment which has ceilings as high as a court-
house where we meet your lover who has white hair and
a slight paunch and I write you off for trading me for
him, only I don't say it out loud, and he says he's glad
I'm around to take care of Jamie weekends while he takes
you off to the woods, and I say don't count on it, I only
used to be your friend and stomp out knowing it is not
your moving that puts me in this rage, but the shifting of
your loyalty to a fat old man who won't let you call me or
meet me for lunch or come for dinner with just Jamie and
then it leaps up inside me like a salmon from an icy place
that he is neither fat nor old but young and blond, and a
pain too familiar stiffens my body so I can't wake, can't
forget. It is a lover you have taken from me, who takes
you from me, takes you to a street I can't get to, takes you
into his bed, lights candles, disconnects the phone,
absorbs you like clay does water, (you filling his pores,
he, a canyon holding you in,) and me desolate as Utah.

ARGUING WITH JOYCE

We are all out there on the edge with parachutes
and it is no picnic and the edge keeps moving
towards us and receding again until the eyes and
the feet and the stomach have no guarantee they're
related. There is only one rule, you can't move
backwards, so it's only a question of whether the
edge will meet you before you meet it. Any
woman who yells, *no one understands!* is a fool.
There is no woman who doesn't understand.
It is a prism of understanding. You stand on an
edge that cuts while I stand on a surface that burns,
you stand on Route 128 unable to move your car
yelling to the rain which is deaf as well as mute
and I yell to the strep in my daughter's throat
which makes a statement of pus. Either way,
no one arrives on a white horse, no one even sends
help. You call for a tow and hitch to work
drenched, I stay at home for the fourth day
in a row. The edge wavers again. When it finally
happens, nothing will matter. Your Saab with its
cracked block, nursing my daughter back to health,
getting your budget in before June, getting my
poems out before I land, forgetting to write our
wills. It all happened so fast, we'll say, We saw it
coming for years, the race, the edge, the air, the free
fall, this falling free and we are all howling
in the green air. Howling with laughter.

VIEWS FROM FLIGHT 485

Blue eyes sits in 25, my row, flying East
across America: blue eyes with lashes like
evergreens in a dark forest face--even
the stewardess remarks. Blue eyes will
keep me safe, aloft, so to speak, he takes
out his map, we speculate on what route
the pilot flies by the shapes of fields,
the rise in terrain, fans and meanders
of rivers; blue eyes has the pilot trace
our path. I'm mesmerized. We review
the meal, we chat: his dad blasts high -
way cuts, and he develops housing tracts.
He is nineteen or twenty-five; I barely
think of dying. The plane is flying smooth
as Kezar Lake on a windless day, doesn't
matter that I'm middle aged. I say,
those highway cuts, geologists' delights,
reveal how our earth evolved. Then blue
eyes shows his book about the Scope's Trial,
says some people actually believe in
evolution, he's incredulous. I nod, intuit
turbulence ahead; he shows me pages where
the ACLU favors Communists, abortionists.
He flaps his lashes, innocent creationist.
No good, blue eyes! Your inside's gush.
I think of mid-air crashes, failing landing
gear, I'm forty-three again, wingless
evolutionist abandoned to the air.

Waiting in Line at the Bank

is a test they never tell you about in the fifth
grade. For the occasion they close down two
of the windows, the man at the head of the line
has saved all his transactions from the whole
year for this moment, and the teller takes this
chance to learn to type. Christmas is upon us,
all the crap in the stores awaits this money
that is not forthcoming. Go home, then, make
a fire, write a poem, up-end the rituals and
expectations you are trapped in, let the tellers
out of their cages and into the lobbies to dance,
let the sullen manager open the bulletproof
vaults to the citizens, let the citizens get what
they came for quickly and without guns, let
the spirit of giving prevail, oh hail, oh hell
bankers, let the computers go down for a change
in peace, let the balances rise up like flames
of Chanukah candles, like stars of Bethlehem,
like hallelujahs out of the mouths of children.

POETRY READINGS

It is war, and the poets who want merely to read to their
handful of sincere followers in a space as quiet as a vault,
are losing. Upstairs a band's disco base strangles the delicate
rhythms of each poem. In the street, a jackhammer breaks up
the pavement at 9 p.m. jangling each image until it shatters
and fails. There is every possible emergency: fires, coronaries,
police chasing burglars who never considered larceny until
this poem and sirens competing as if a poet were a serious
contender. The subway, even blocks away, rumbles wildly,
and the underworld shudders. In the square, there are fist
fights, vandals gather at the windows of the shops banging,
for what? an earthen pot? a fabric notebook? a poet in the
midst of a sestina to come out and fight? This is nothing.
An old woman with a bag walks to the front of the room
and shouts "This stinks!" waving her bag at the poet who
cringes behind a page. Find me the room where words shape
themselves in air, drift like specks of dust into a stream of light
and out again, where poems spin like silk, in silence,
clothing you in the finest garment there is.

THREE

It is a question of timing.

IT IS A QUESTION OF TIMING

and when as a young girl, I wanted to put your hand on my
breast, your hair was too long and people gaped at you even
in Harvard Square. And when you left school and begged me
to come along like a gypsy on a Harley, I fled to my dorm at
Wellesley and crossed my legs. And when you pulled up,
a year later, with a full brown beard and a Mexican dress for me,
I was away healthy at camp with twelve ten-year olds who
thought I was Mother Superior, stable as Gibraltar, I lectured
you, trying to rid you of your shrinks, your demons, intense
as I could be for a day at a time, until I started to giggle, horri-
fied you'd discover the real me. Oh your hand was strong by
the wide Susquehanna and your voice saying your poems was
deeper than your years. Now you arrive, left by your wife and
kids, to me, left as a wife with my kids, charming in your
Pakistani coat, your fluid Spanish, your rakish hat, the crowsfeet
warming your eyes, your voice resonant as night, your laugh
a comet. How have you come at the perfect time, at the sun's
eclipse, taking my breath like an orange moon rising? How
have you come in the month - long blizzard to wrap yourself
around my children on their sled? How have you stayed with
your white wine buried in snow outside my window, my raw
hands warming under your fleecy coat, our foreheads rubbing
away their creases, and finally, after twenty years, our tongues.

MAY DAY

I wanna call you all the names, baby honey, sweet love, darling,
sugarpie, rosehips, apricot lips, I wanna laugh so it's so far down
in my belly you feel it through your lovable dick up through your
groin until your epiglottis wags with joy, hey honey, don't need
no lunch when I got you, don't need no bath, the odors we put out
have them forming lines to see what we got cooking, everything coming
out of our kitchen, hot and earthy stew, epicurean soufflé, Long
Island duckling even, give me your leg , you take the delicate rise
near my breast, this is the first of May and if it wasn't raining
so hard, we'd be loving it up under that tree, and the whole earth'd be
pushing up against that perfect ass of yours, pine needles sticking in
your crack, smells we'd longed for all winter, dirt on my knees, worms
wondering what the fuss is overhead, everything steamy as if an eruption
were imminent, our mouths busy planting and in our heads, the crops,
corn, alfalfa, jungles of beans applauding our recognition of the day.

THE ORIGIN OF CABBAGE

I drove over to Buzzels for some fresh corn and there
was a cabbage so big and healthy looking, I had to buy it,
75¢ and it weighed probably six pounds easy. I don't
even like cabbage but this one made you want to like it,
pale green and shiny like someone had just polished it,
and veins like on the forearm of a construction worker,
it seemed like just one leaf, the outer one, had built
a whole town with no help, the outer edge of this outer
leaf curled over in a sort of wide open grin and peeling
that leaf back, another with its own creeks, tributaries
and deltas, I swear the whole damn Mississippi lives in
this next leaf, and the next one, just slightly paler,
and the next one a bit more tender and ruffled a little
like a grown woman in gowns and so on, the whole thing
packed and dense, couldn't get more food than this into
a ball, it feels good just to hold it under your arm.
So I bring this cabbage home and admire it for a while,
showing it off to friends as if I'd given birth to it
and it does seem unlikely that a thing like a cabbage
could just grow out of the ground rather than condensing
say, into a cool green planet in orbit around the sun.

THE DAY THE TELESCOPE

The day the telescope arrived, the light
hung on forever; you had to point it at
the harbor, the towers, planes, the cars
crawling painfully down the central artery
until the sun set. You forgot food, drove
to the darkest park in town, screwed it
to its tripod, silver stars etched onto
the dome of your mind. Chanting the co-
ordinates, you prepare now to let go
of time. You put your eye to the lens
and the haze moves apart: Polaris, Castor,
tiny points of light grow round and split
into double stars that fold back if you
squint too hard; and the great Nebula
of Orion blossoms out like breath on an
icy morning. Focus in, Sirius moves across
the field too quickly, you feel the earth
spinning, you rock back, forget the cold,
the cops flashing their blue lights at you,
shouting, "the park is closed!" through
their bullhorns. Not the skies, ancient
as they are, they open to you for the first
time. From the oyster of the heavens,
you pluck star clusters, pearly gray,
edging the Milky Way. Carefully, you locate
a galaxy, beyond ours, its photons of light
left its spiral arms so long ago, holding
the oldest secrets of our birthing, and barrel
toward you certain you'll be prepared, you'll
dare to look up at the moment that particular
photon needs to be seen, to slip into an eye,
yours, open wider than it ever was, like the
ear of a deaf person who suddenly hears; it
would be no surprise at all if your soul
leapt out through your iris, shuttled the
tunnels of the telescope building up speed
and shot out, lighting up the day time sky,
in search of a wilder dwelling.

SEARCHING FOR THE LAST QUARK
DOWN AT THE TAM

We're waiting on Leon Collins to tap out a little jazz down
here at the Tam O'Shanter on Monday evening, and you say
one teaspoon of the neutron star at the center of the Crab Nebula
would weigh a trillion tons and were we to fall off this very table
like our bottle of beer to that star only a meter away, we'd be
traveling two million miles an hour when we hit. We sip a little
Miller's and think on it. The boys are setting up their amps,
Leon comes in, skinny old black man wearing his hair like a
hat. You say, *when we look through the near side of Andromeda's*
galaxy to the far, we're looking back 100,000 years through time
watching the very evolution, the making of that galaxy, observing
from our front porch, the fourth dimension. I say, where's Leon?
My sitter has to leave at ten. I gotta get up at seven to teach,
and *this neighbor, Glashow, you say, is searching for the Truth,*
the name he's given to the sixth and last quark, which if he finds it,
will put it all together at last. Remember Les McCann banging
away at the Truth on his upright, grunting and groaning as
if those notes held all the secrets. You say, *when our sun's*
time is up, we'll finish as a cold white dwarf. No exotic super-
nova spewing us out into the cosmos to seed new stars. Uhuh, our
future holds no glamor. Come on Leon, we need you now.
My kids made my time span shrink. I measure my tenure in
this universe by what size clothes they're on and how often
they talk about sex. *We're made, though, of the same stuff as*
stars, stardust. We were cooked up in that same hot cauldron that
busted out all that junk we gaze at. Well that's a little more
cheery. And Leon, he comes clickety-clicking out onto the
floor boards, easy as dreaming on stars, with his gals in gold
pants, heel-ball-toeing their bluesy routines, putting silence
like a white flash in the middle of the tappety sound, syn-
chronized, cool as quarks, making a kind of physics
of the soul.

How We Came to Earth

Lisa said there'd be falling stars tonight so we all went
down to the dock with foam pads and sleeping bags, pillows
flashlights, Jo wanted to know if she could take her old
teddy, I mean it wasn't exactly spontaneous, all this
preparation, just to take five adults twenty feet down
to the dock. We spread it all out and lay down and covered
ourselves up with a quilt, we were like a big sandwich
filled with sardines. There were a few distant lights of
cottages, but other than that, just stars, skillions of them
and that crazy froth of the Milky Way pouring into the pines
by the shore. Stars did shoot, mostly out of the Big Dipper,
etching their bright tails into the night, you'd kind of
catch it out of the corner of your eye, or maybe miss
it altogether trying to figure out what they could have possibly
meant when they drew a hunter around three meagre stars.
Anyway, you'd feel the star falling through the body tensed
next to you, as if we were all one creature, the only one
under these huge heavens to witness such burning, ten eyes
glowing up out of the lake, where we'd fallen too.

FISHING

From my view in the lake, the whole shore is rather dark,
the deep green of August, our brown cottage barely visible
through the mossy trunks of pines. Only a few bolts of birch
spark the foliage and you, in your gold chamois shirt and beige
panama hat, standing on the dock shedding light like a dog
shaking water. Casting, reeling in, casting again, as if what
you were fishing for was not bass or perch, but a rhythm and
peace you have already caught. You peer into the lake looking
for signs, the right temperature and depth, a few sheltering
lily pads.

This is what I'm doing too, my line arcing inward with a slow
wssshh casting for words or simply shadow and light. Dreaming on
the glitter of words, as the spinner draws through water. I cast,
and if I can be patient as an angler, the bait catches me. Who
fishes and who is hooked? That bass you long for, that may never
even nibble, let alone strike, is playing you. I'm on the end
of the line sensing its tugs and pulls. Your bass teases. It
never feeds before storms, or when the lake is calm. Or ruffled.
Or when there is too much light. Or before dawn. At dinner,
(we are eating steak), your bass calls. They're biting now!
you shout on the way to the dock. I look out. Words leap and
smack the surface. Breathcatching.

GEM

I love that old man up on Hurricane Mountain
who has his rocks out for sale on rickety
saw-horse tables in his front yard, on a road
almost nobody travels, and those who do,
probably live there and don't need to buy
his rocks, they've got plenty of their own,
so he just sits there overweight and wheezing,
with rosy quartz and mica, geodes and slices
of talc, a few crystals from Brazil, he says,
semi-precious, garnet and topaz. And he'll
tell you he picked lots of these stones right
off Hurricane Mountain, where they were nothing,
just old gray stones you'd kick at, only he
polished and cut them, until they are speckled
and sleek as leopards, until their hidden seams
rise up like deltas, until they draw you in
and down like water where fish startle and gleam.
Just holding one, you slip past the surface of
things, down the silvery veins of the mind.

Giving Over Control

Sometime during the interval of anesthesia when time
according to Einstein is stopped by the gravity of
the situation, an incision is made in a woman, decisions
leapt to by teams of technicians who can't see past her
body to the cinnamon of her life, her fuchsias and velvets,
her children with yellow hair, songs, and mother in
heaven, father by the sea, prayers, beloved friends
who pace in the lounge where time, oddly enough, heaves
by like an old covered wagon. Under the glaring light,
it is merely a bare belly framed by sheets. And the
woman, who was last seen directing everything in sight,
who layered her sterile hospital room with art and poems,
charms of great power, who hummed through the long
responsible corridors, is now amorphous as amnesia,
her aging has stopped for an hour, her chronology
rests deeply, her mind is busy elsewhere, in a former
or after life, gliding among stars or starfish.
She has no say, is under the watchful eye
of beads and prophets, under the charged spell
of those who love her. The clean scar
on her body will be read as a rune,
a glyph, a brief skip in her lifeline.

WORLD SERIES 1986

He walks in the door. The game is about to begin.
He will not hear the closing bars of the anthem,
the rising cheer before "home of the brave," he
will not see the opening plays. He is changing
clothes. Off with the suit, on with the lucky
pants, lucky shirt, lucky sweater, and where
are the lucky socks. The socks! This is a grown
man, Phi Beta Kappa from Brown, a man who
reads *Sky and Telescope*, who can describe the
most recent theory of the universe, who has some
grasp of a quantum leap, this man lies down
in front of the tube and carefully crosses his left
leg over his right. He is drinking the right beer,
the one that won the play-offs, keeping score
with the only pencil that will call up a reverse K
from the blank white box and everywhere,
reasonable citizens, families with logical lives,
students who know the Laws of Physics, Nobel
Prize winners, anthropologists, are poking their
caps inside out, switching them backwards,
throwing the vibrating cat out of the only chair
that works. *Magic. Magic.* How far we've come
from the flinging of salt over the shoulder, from
the chanting in the mouth of the cave to bring
the hunter his prey; one square of pavement
toward the next crack--*step on it, break your
mother's back.* For if we lose, it will be the fault of
the missing socks. But if we win, we will forget
the incantations and the outfits we wore, we will
remember the brave knees of Buckner and the
sliding curves of Hurst, we will think that
we deserved it, we of the bleeding hearts,
of the hearts too battered to bear even the next
pitch.

FOUR

So much of my life crowds in on me here.

BLACKOUT

It all started when the pipes froze. Well maybe not.
It all started when the furnace broke and we were
huddled around the wood stove trying to survive.
Then the pipe burst and water, as in Niagara Falls,
roared down through all four stories of our house.
That's what I love about January! The phone went
dead, the only aspect of this crisis my daughter
even noticed. Things continued in this vein. The
plumber came once and never returned, and the
adjuster called to cancel three times. Now by some
miracle, he is here, looking like a minister in Ver-
mont, dark-suited and spare, a just adjuster.
It is four p.m., minutes before dark. We start
in the attic, tracing the damage the water has done,
inspect the third floor, descend to the second.
The lights go out. We blink, straining to see where
the hall ceiling is about to fall. I peer into
the graying street. BLACKOUT. Who could have
thought this up? The children are running around
frantic without their tape decks and TVs.
Naturally, the adjuster leaves. I light some
Shabbas candles, signifying rest, signifying peace.
They disappear in little hands. Candles in every
room of this old ark. I can't keep track and one
spark is all it takes. I am trying to carry on by flame,
fold the clothes, fix the meal, but when I check,
the kids have put a candle in a dish and are feeding
it with paper scraps as if it were a gerbil.
I whisk the blaze to the kitchen just as the glass
cracks. Wax, glass, and water flood the room.
How sweet these blackouts, how cozy, like in the
olden days, ma. Fire and ice. Ice and fire.
The world ends maybe three times a month;
maybe twice, begins.

WESTPORT ISLAND, MAINE

The first summer my husband can't leave town.
The kids are toddlers. The cottage is doll size.
Miniature everything: rooms, steps, kitchen, windows;
we barely wedge ourselves in. It is on the banks
of the Sheepscot. This is before I know about tides,
I mean I know in theory, but in practice, I have
a ways to go. The ad read: Cottage Walking Distance
To Beach. It is noon. I pack the kids' supplies:
food, bottles, diapers, towels, blankets, I need
a camel-train. Caroline, though, helps me lug them
down. The path is marginal, it opens and falls away
along the ridge high above the river. Bushwhacking
with babies, I call it. We sidestep down a ragged
trail and find, beyond the weeping birches and the rim
of sand, a cove, a lovely cove of mud, black oozing mud.
I am confused. Where's the water? the children wail.
I close my eyes and tug at my mind like a moon.
What I know about tides, about the steep banks
of tidal rivers, finally arrives. I check my watch.
It'll be back, I say at six. No swimming today.
And we truck back, the kids livid with disappointment,
and me, relieved the local folks, Greenleaf and Whittier,
are out of sight. So we learn about moon, current, and
tide. Whole bodies of water, people even, leave us
and return, and leave. It is out of our control.
We can watch the empty space, longing for it to fill
or find what is there already, deep in the shelter
and wonder of mud.

X-RATED

One morning in the cottage in Maine when the fog
that lay over the lake was thick enough to keep secrets
and I lay pretending to be asleep, I heard giggles from
where the kids, two boys and a girl, were supposed to be
sleeping, a whispering loud enough to lift the fog...*do it,
do it, is it in?...I think so...well is it?...yep it is...oh you're
doing it, you're doing it, what does it feel like...* and later with
the loons calling through the mist and the cook stove
kindled, one of the boys says...*should we tell her...
yea...no...tell her...oh no don't...Tell me what?* I say wanting
to hear it from the culprit's mouth...*He put his dinky in her
you know what...*shouted the terrified observer, the one
who rooted from the sidelines, who egged on the small
explorers with vicarious joy. *No!...said the culprit...I was
only kidding, I couldn't get it in, I just said I did...*the child
already pressured by his peers to keep it up even before
"up" is a possibility and the boys spending hours meas-
uring their dicks in second grade, an overwhelming
concern for length, while the girl, outnumbered, yes,
but hardly victimized, making herself available as a
dandelion, a forecast of glorious events to come.
Oh god help the parents who have run out of guides
through this unlikely wilderness.

LOW TIDE

So much of my life crowds in on me here in the small stone
cottage where we vacation, two adults and four children,
hardly restful, that the slim space where words sometimes
bloom has closed like an eyelid and there is only me and
the chaos which appears to be mine. Oh yes, I can use
words to speak to the children about how they must not fall
into the sea or what they will eat or why they must not light
fires in their bedrooms or shout swears across the peaceful
family land, and I can use words to ask my man what he will
do today, the simplest exchanges, but as far as describing
how I feel or my annoyance at the tide's restlessness, it is
impossible. These words have drained out like the water
from our bay. I cannot swim at the hottest time, all the rocks
and mud laid bare. I stare at the tight beaks of barnacles
which keep the life moist inside and at the incautious hollow
ones which opened on the ebbing tide. What is the lesson?
Wait. Do not make conclusions based on what will surely
change. It is not the end of art or love. Just low tide.
A twice daily phenomenon the sea puts up with, its life
seething below the unglamorous mud. The tide will
come in. Feelings will seep into the marsh grass.
And words, real ones, the ones that prickle and swim,
will lap at the doorstep again.

AT THE LAKE WITHOUT KIDS

I have not made breakfast for anyone and am swimming far
out into the lake, naked as a salamander. No one is screaming,
ma come back, where's my bathing suit. I can hear the loons for
once. On the dock, you are casting great sinuous curves, your
lures rising as high as the mountains. No children are waiting
for their turns squabbling over who is supposed to be next to
tangle the fancy flies in the lily pad stems. I climb out and
smooth the water from my breasts. Allure is stronger than
desire to fish and the bass can wait. Right on the deck, under
the great white pines, you cast in the hot deep place and a
whole body comes shuddering up on your line. No one is
shouting, *ooh, they're humping!* Bees, loud as motor boats,
watch out for us, for a change, and the lake gleams silver. We
forget lunch and stare for some time at the space between two
ranges where the highest peak might appear. We speculate on
clouds. No one is whining, *I'm bored. What should we do?* We
do all the nothing we want and forget to shop. Oh well. At
seven, we take our cocktails to the old wood love seat at the
beach. Swallows skip off the water like small stones. No one
is shouting, *I'm starving, let's eat!*. The sun melts like raspberry
sherbet over the lake and sky. The birches bend down to peer
at themselves in the still water. We do not move until the first
star appears. At dinner, no one asks, *What's for dessert?* Hot
raspberry pie with cream, as it turns out. *We have not forgotten
we have them. They are on our minds in a way that accentuates the
peace.* We sleep outside in case a star falls. We don't have to
miss a thing. Inside, no one is having nightmares and has to
be held. We wrap around each other, as if we weren't parents,
exhausted and tense. As if we were people with genitals and
hearts.

LOOKING FOR CAMP TO-HO-NE

We found it when we had literally given up, driven
around the perimeter of Lake Buel several times and
taken almost every dirt road down to the shore. The old
grounds keeper at one camp, the wrong one, said your
camp was closed, your sign down. What would it be,
we wondered, a trailer site, an Evangelical Bible Camp, a
Psychotherapeutic Retreat. By the time we gave up, we'd
seen every little cottage on the lake, had our toes and spit
bitten by sunnies, those herds of fish that turn the lake to
chowder, guaranteed the need for a new muffler for the
abused bottom of the car. It was dusk when you shouted
"What's that!" We parked in the oval, high with ragweed
and yarrow. Your old camp, abandoned, the log bunks
sturdy as when you left twenty-eight years ago, some of
their doors ajar, the mildly rotted docks pulled up near
their moorings, the lodge, that ark of a structure where
you sang the *Pirates of Penzance*, sagging, lost. You
wanted so desperately to find this camp, you make it into
symbols. No changes in life but crumbling. That's
wrong. This place has a beauty we all want, a sense of
our youth, but with crow'sfeet and ease. What loomed so
large, rituals and campfires, paths that led to some
desirable haunt, off-limit to the kids, each rock you
scuffed on the way to the dock, still exist surrounded by a
silence only years of memory can preserve. We examine
every corner, we wade through the grasses and the
woods. You have the best of it, believe me, this camp is
completely yours.

NIGHTS UNDER THE TRUMPET VINE

I am on the second bench with Lyla, splinters
digging into our thighs, rows of girls in camp
shorts behind us and the lights of the show on
the stage stunning the moths and swallows who fly
out of the black night. Over us, the trumpet vine
hangs its long orange blossoms. We pull them
from their vine. We fit trumpet flowers over
each finger and pretend our wild orange nails could
hurt the air. We tickle each other's arms with
trumpet fingers, like delicate legs of spiders.
We toot into the small end, making a section
of horns. We put our tongues deep in the hollows
to find the honey of the stamen, that place the
bees sing to all the hot day. We strip the velvet
petals back past colors of rust to fruit orange
to rind of lemon. When the play ends, the delicate
blooms, what we have loved and desired, are in tatters
around us, the petals like flakes of dawn. We return
to our bunks, yawning, stained, not with guilt
for the damage we've done, but with trumpet honey
and the clear hot notes of sun.

PARADE

If a small town has nothing but the Fourth of July, it has a
lot. A parade, forming since dawn in rows and lines that
stretch through three towns, the line is that long, the towns,
that small. A parade with every convertible, float, hearse,
every marching band in the state, every official, Miss Amer-
ica, the mayor, the governor, the sanitary engineers driving
their green trucks, clowns, firemen, their axes gleaming,
unicycle riders peddling backwards and forwards teetering
on the peaks of their hoops, veterans of every war, holding
their every breath in suits, every Boy Scout of every troop,
their leaders, their den mothers, flags, banners, bagpipes,
flutes, tubas, ranks of tubas like elephant ears marching, like
plumbers, kilts, sabres, cannons, bombs, great steaming
horses bred for parades, for this one day, plumed like
pecaderos, a platoon of cameras recording every mile of this
strange river, dragging fringe from its banks, children
stamping and humming on porches, in elms, on shoulders,
under legs, the beating of drums, snare drums, bass drums,
cymbals, triangles, bells, pregnant women hold their bellies
afraid of vibrating into labor, and every union, every em-
ployer, every girl from two to twenty in skirts, in shorts, in
glittering cuffs and hats and boots, twirling batons they've
twirled since birth, the Senior Twirlers, painted and panting,
the Youth division shifting position like geese in a chevron,
the Toddler Twirlers, propped up by an edge of mothers
who spray them with water to keep them like roses, while
the tar softens under July sun and the parade begins at noon
or one when the mayor arrives fresh from lunch and nods,
the line moves forward in slow swells of hot, tired fathers
and soldiers and children who look at the dirty kids in bare
feet on the curbs without curls without lipstick without
batons, at the sticky kids licking lemon popsicles, and the
parade moves, its musical dirge celebrating their
independence.

RELIGION

I am in the old *shul* between the railroad and the glass
factory and on the *bima* Mr. Goldberg is racing Mr. Horowitz
through the *ovenus*. They are both half deaf. Their prayers
live in them like salt and when they *doven*, the prayers pour
out. Uncle Ben and Uncle Wolf have their own books, each
a little different, and their own tunes and their own wives
whispering about their own menopauses. *L'cha adonai
hagdula* the old rabbi sings bringing the torah down the
steps, down the aisle, slowly shuffling toward me and
Andra in the back row, where the slatted seats are biting our
bottoms. We hold our giggles in our throats with our palms,
he's here and we kiss our fingertips and touch the torah,
he's gone up the other aisle and up the steps. The prayers
resume as a train screams by drowning out all Judaism. Mr.
Goldberg doesn't flinch, his chants are soundless. It is a long
one, we count the cars by their click and picture oranges and
trucks stacked up and slats with cows between and rolls of
glinting steel, our giggles free now like doves in the sooty
brick sanctuary until the last car, the eighty-seventh, when
the chanting emerges like entrails from a train. Tomorrow
we will kiss Billy in the basement after Sunday School if the
New York Express doesn't shake us loose. These were the
years I knew the motions but not the words, a religion tied
up with the B & O, a sacred scroll connected to Billy Felder's
lips, the old men reliable and insistent as the roar that shook
our *shul*.

FIVE

One evening when I was busy typing, my daughter turned.

ONE EVENING WHEN I WAS BUSY TYPING, MY DAUGHTER

turned from a large rather chunky disheveled
fourth grade girl into something more like an
adult with a kind of waist and hair flipped
back under barrettes and much to say about sex
and boys, my own extravagances and trespasses
such as showing my neckline unnecessarily low,
oh boy, no part of my body should show even when
I bathe, even when it's only my daughter looking.
She surprised me like someone vaguely familiar
stepping from an elevator I might be waiting for,
a distant relative from another town, a person
you wouldn't mistake for a child. An arrival
I wasn't prepared for though someone announced
it long ago. I sneak looks in the bathroom
at her thickening pubic hair. I stand by her
while she sleeps, her body using most of the
bed now, and see where boys will warm to her
roundnesses, will rub their new stubble over
her sensuous cheeks.

How He Won the War

You know how you get after teaching all day. The Great Gift-
giver. Tired. We are eating french toast, all I am up to for
dinner, and my kids are laughing, getting sillier and sillier,
getting gross in fact, popping up and down in their chairs eating
bananas in suggestive ways, using salt shakers for testicles and
boobs, so I set my mouth in the "grim look" the one I usually use
for meals to keep the lid on, I say, Sit down, we're going to eat a
nice peaceful dinner, but they've finished, and Shauna suddenly
remembers *La Cucaracha* and some Spanish besides, and she's
dancing around the table, Davey leaps up and joins in, only now
the words are *La Cockarocha* something they've learned at camp,
it seems, and they are doing this calypso number, bumping hips,
bumping asses, dancing wildly, laughing and taking flying leaps,
it's clear someone will crash into a door and need stitches so I
keep my lips straight, I keep that grown-up person on my face,
that mask I wear that's almost part of me now, it reminds kids
that I'm tired, but clearly it does not remind them to calm down,
my daughter is waggling her womanly hips, my son, just half her
size, is falling and springing up and suddenly I smile, I can
actually feel my skin crack, it's all so ridiculous, and my son
stops dead. *She's smiling,* he says. *She's smiling!* he yells as if all
this ranting and heat were meant to make one thing happen. He
runs to hug me hard as if he's won the war, David against the
Goliath of my life, David with his sling of humor, his small well-
aimed stones of joy.

CRIME

"Practice!" I yell from my study to my daughter, "the recital's tomorrow." "But I can't," she whines, "I can't find the rosin." "Well look under your bed, "I yell back." I did and it's not there and now I can't practice, listen to this..."and she scrapes the catgut across the strings like nails on a blackboard, only a small bit worse than the usual sound. "Then wait," I say wanting to finish a poem, and by the time I go finally to hunt the rosin, something glistens on the bow, something that never met catgut before and the top of the Vaseline jar is off, an unhealthy a sign as there can be for a violin. "You didn't!" I say stroking my finger down the greasy bow, dabbing the gobs of petroleum jelly on the strings.

Sometimes it is a small thing that drives a mother to murder. For a few minutes, locked in my own room to keep myself from violence, I couldn't tell if this was a small incident or the Bay of Pigs. No recital, and I would have to admit to someone, the teacher, the tolerant music store that rents these tiny instruments, that my daughter saw fit to coat her strings with Vaseline, the new rosin substitute. A lifetime of savings to replace the gooey violin, the end of music, of all art for that matter, but by midnight I am laughing over the heinous crime and my wildly inventive kin, relieved to have averted death of the first born due to violin.

THE FINAL GAME

Her son is at bat, most of the rainy spring season behind
him. He looks like every other seven or eight year old out
there, jeans and navy team shirt. He has a special crouch
today, having discovered only minutes before the game
begins, he has a rip in the back of his pants. In the field, he
stretches his t-shirt down over his butt and gnaws at his
mitt, another singular trait. Now he's taking warm-up
swings, chewing his sugarless Bubbleyum like the pros,
eyeing the ball, tense. The mothers and fathers, ex-hus-
bands, visiting aunts, old teachers and egads, friends,
are waiting to cheer for their tikes at their first real
game..."three strikes yer out" this time and the pitch comes
from the hand of his best friend's dad and he swings as if
he's swatting a fly in the kitchen. The mother is chatting
equal time with her boyfriend and the father of her son, it is
a delicate situation and the son sways back from home plate
letting the ball pass like a bull. The mother doesn't care if he
strikes out, she assures another parent, but he's worked
these two months following John of Infinite Patience, the
coach, like a guru and he finally knows how to hold his
glove, to field a grounder and keep his butt low to the
ground and scuttle sideways across the infield like a crab,
and which way to run, if not exactly when and what the
ultimate goal of this slow summer ritual really is. This could
be anywhere in America in June and the spectators in each
field are as connected to each other as blood relatives at this
minute when the third pitch meets the bat and the boy,
astonished as he is sure, reaches first base to cheers that
would make an observer think that everything hinged on
this one small feat. Everything does. The boy leaps into the
air with joy, the mother remarks that all the inconveniences
of the season were worth it, and the father remembers his
youth. The game ends, the parents cheer the coach, the
children clutch their certificates to their hearts and flushed
with wanting everything, Big Macs, love and the wild
cheering of crowds, they wander out of the park into their
next season.

VISITING DAY

He's playing soccer when I arrive, goalie, in fact, and I sense
that he senses me, but he won't let down his guard until the
scrimmage ends. He runs in slow motion toward me. I run.
We hug. He's back to the game. How will I kidnap my
child away from all these feats of prowess? The parents are
clumped like uneven hedges along the sidelines, trying to be
interested, to be pleased, smiling, pointing to their boy in
blue (they're all in blue) who's just kicked his teammate
instead of the ball, all their packages, gifts and briskets,
jawbreakers and taffy stacked on the warm, trod grass.
Later, we tuck ourselves onto the lower bunk bed on that flat
mattress he probably wets and count the loot. We try the
trampoline, bouncing into the air, one hovering, while the
other laughs, collapsing. Shooting baskets, he tells me how
to make it rebound, swish, and dunk, returning the ball to
me over and over as if I were the camper and he, my dad.
He wants my picture down on "fishing rock", but when I
pose, he says, "No, be real!" We dangle our legs into the
lake. He points to the island where they camp. "There's a
granite ledge", he says, "I run to all day long for the view.
It looks like a loon lake, mom, but there are none". After all,
some small part of this child is mine. We feel the tug of the
thin invisible line. Visiting ends. We part at the ball field
where we met. I touch his hair. It's yellowed over the ears
and where it's damp and pushed up, his pale skin makes a
rim around the tan. His small boy kiss. He turns back. The
weeks of expectation reduced to three sticks of Bubbleyum
in his fist. I fumble for my key. There are two cars and a
base line between my son and me. This is just the beginning.
He walks back into his own life, pitching and dribbling,
listening for distant loons.

Initiation at Bash Bish Falls

Here's the scene. Thirty tourists are perched on the rocks
surrounding the pool. A hundred feet over us a thin stream
thrusts through the glacial debris, and spews, like a distant
ejaculation into the icy green. Four teenage boys are at the
upper lip of the falls meditating on this phenomenon. Six
teenage boys, their girls sunning beside them, are standing
to my right. A sign says, *No Dogs and No Swimming.* A boy
drops out of the sky. He edged from terror into air at the
moment I noticed a lap dog yapping. Another boy leaps.
The crowd cheers relieved it's not them having to step into
nothing but roar. The kids go wild. The lithe girls shift for
an even tan. Their boyfriends gaze wide-mouthed at their
peer, speeding like a particle of light toward the watery
glass. Smack and he's into the next phase, terror subsumed
in cold. Who knows what he sees in the dim basin that
swallows froth. When he surfaces chattering, the tourists
scan his face for hints of pain. He can't let on. By the third
leap, the boys by me, my greenhorns, know they will have to
jump. They are rocking from foot to foot. They are mutter-
ing words that egg each other on. They are getting ready to
leave, to climb the steep ledges hand over hand,
to hover at great length at the border of brook and spume.
There is no choice. While the mothers imagine them draped
at Lambert's drinking Coke, their sons plummet into man-
hood and almost all of them survive.

JOHN'S STORY

You think your teenage kid is bad, when I was thirteen,
I fell in love with a girl at camp, we used to sneak away
and do it. After camp, I suffered, lost weight, essentially
I was wasting away from love, I understood heartbreak,
it was clear I'd have to make my way to Queens where this
girl Sandy lived. Ten thirty was my curfew, no way my
parents would let me go. I had this bike trip scam, I was
leaving early Saturday, cycling Boston's suburbs or the
south shore coast. I left by the window the night before,
took the night train to New York City, hopped off at Grand
Central, caught the local to Queens and this girl had found
some barn we could meet in, spend the day in each other's
arms among cow patties and tractors, and I was home,
back in my parents' house in Quincy by ten at night, my
friends covered for me, and I did this maybe four, five
times and was never caught, by my folks at least. Once
though the cops surrounded the barn where we lay in the
proverbial hay; someone saw us trespass and suspected we
were a couple of kids who'd just held up the local grocery,
so the cops came in with guns, we had our hands up over
our heads, I mean my parents didn't even know I was in
New York, let alone in some barn being frisked, one cop
puts us in his car, he's going to take us in to book us, I can't
be booked, what am I going to tell my folks, so while he's
walking around the car from closing Sandy in the back seat,
I say to Sandy, "Jump! Split!" "Four at the clock by Ed's,"
she says and we make the break. I know this cop is not
going to chase her, so I fly out leaping fences, he's after me
for sure, but I'm in shape, a track star to be honest; I can't
remember if he actually fires, maybe it's my pulse, but I
lose him and Sandy's there at four by the clock at Ed's, and
that's how I led my life when I was thirteen and that wasn't
half of it.

WHAT THEY REMEMBER

You'd think a bright June day at the beach, a day where
the breeze lifts the edge of your beach towel and the girls press
their oiled bodies into the topography of sand, moving their
lovely hips and shoulders to the voice which emanates
insistently from the red plastic box, you'd think a day
you could walk up the tidal inlets and actually see snails
walking around imperceptibly slow with antenna sculpting
the air, a day sails wedged open the dark blue sky, would stay
in a young mind; you'd think a day you ate buckets of sweet
clams by the Essex River where old dories leaned over in the
salty mud, a day you hopped over boulders while the sun spread
its deep fluorescence over Gloucester Harbor, Ten Pound Island
heavy with gulls and the Dog Bar Light winking through the
crystal dusk, a day like that would be an old familiar painting
on the walls of the mind forever, framed maybe by the ride home
with everyone too crisp to touch, too hot to be in heat, cousins
from distant cities, crammed into the back seats, giggling over
accents and local figures of speech. But no. What they loved
was the breakdown on Storrow Drive, a truck wedged into a
tunnel too low for its passage, and the traffic at a dead halt, folks
emerging from cars like stunned mayflies in the sweet darkness
by the Charles River, drivers inching slowly backwards, daring
to imagine they might back down the expressway, actually
turning their cars around so cars were stuck at every angle on
the three lane road, a letting go of trying to get someplace,
and finally blasting Tina from the tape deck of our car, perfect
strangers dancing and shaking, singing and clapping as if it were
Sunday morning and we were loved and saved.

LEAVING

Our parakeet escaped from the house on the highest day
of spring. Birds across the country warbled with joy.
After the cold winter, after the cramped days inside
its cage or clasped in the hot hands of my daughter
who loved it even more than her bear, our bird knew
this was the day it had to go. For one second the cage
door and the front door were open. That bird streaked
out, made a sharp right across the porch, made another
sharp right (it was used to flying at right angles
from room to room) and flew up through the kitchen
lilac, skimmed the apple frothing with blooms, into
the highest boughs of the silver maple. Paula!
I screamed, leaping into the air like Nureyev, in some
wild hope I could catch her before she left. The fact
of my daughter's loss rose up and stuck. One side of my
heart broke, and the other sped off with the bird
on the most glorious day of her life. High, high
above us, a tiny blue kite streaming across the sky,
barely distinguishable from heaven.

Six

What if you came to the lake for two weeks and the mountains never appeared.

SOLID GROUND;
VIEWS FROM KEZAR LAKE

1

You come down to the lakeside and here it is:
the lowlands, the marshes down by Pigeon Point,
a few small hills, Deer Hill and Ladies' Delight,
the thickly wooded shoreline and Buck Island
jutting from the center of the lake. There are
no clouds, you are simply closed in by white
haze, a softness that washes everything to grays.

2

Another day you push off. You are in a new landscape
altogether. Fierce ranges rise so clearly their spines
show through their vegetation, sun lights each individual
tree, gullies and ridges, charred regions, traces of
clear-cut or blight; you know the people who climb them
are looking out right now toward your cottage, your slice
of silver lake. There is absolutely no question about
these mountains, these ripples your wooden dory makes.

3

Tomorrow there is not a breath. Stillness actually
wakes you. You come to the dock and sunlight leaks
through not from above but from inside the lake as if
someone shone a searchlight from beneath and everything
glitters in an inexplicable way. You are inside the
gentlest place and just beyond your borders, Double-Head,
Speckled, Kearsarge, are shapes of palest gauze.

Drawing By Robert Kroin

4

In this universe, to exist, particles must interact,
be seen, that is a photon of light must come to
something, say an eye, or electron of a tree, a metal
plate or molecule of lake and lo! it registers as light
but otherwise, forget it, traveling through space,
making no waves, pushing nothing aside, it might as well
never have left the point of origin, never have been
flung out into a statistically probable existence.

5

You look out from your porch, naming the mountain you will climb,
you take your maps, compass, backpack, drive through oceans of
potato fields, along the scenic valley road, up through the notch,
and park your car. The trail is steep, you haul your body up, over
roots, boulders, winter debris, up over the ledges, through diminishing
growth. In every patch of sun, blueberries and lovely scarlet laurel.
You are breathless, your legs announce their middle age, your heart
is in temporary shock, and from the peak, you stare out over the
valleys, the ridges, the rivers, across your lake, past Buck Island
and with binoculars, you see your very dock; you might be there
reading magazines or making love, but you are here on this
indisputably lichen-coated granite, capturing it as if it were something
wild, a beast who might escape, gathering its quartz, its berries, its
mica flakes. You lie down on the summit, you are in the sky like a
hawk, the mountain is beneath you, testimony in prehistoric rock.

6

It is dusk. You have returned, your legs quivering beneath you,
able only to rock on the porch and sip tea. The sun sets. Cliffs,
ravines, depressions, what was in front of, what behind, all run
together. You can't distinguish which mountain you've climbed.
You press your quartz and mica in your hand, the haze moves in,
the mountains might be clouds, the familiar face of a deceased,
particles so sparse they don't quite hold, the mist comes up,
the mountains are erased.

7

My mother died. I know this for a fact. I was there
at the funeral. I requested a viewing of the body
before the burial to avoid this confusion. She looked
smaller, not much like my mother, I concede, but her
collar bone pressed up the neckline of her blouse.
Yet she is alive, telling me just now about her golf
game or how I could easily change my life. One night
she emerges from a cavern with her arms outstretched.
She carries bread. It has that yeasty pungent fragrance
of the balsam woods. I know enough not to touch her.
It is lovely. Fine. Tomorrow I am a woman, orphaned,
alone. Today she beckons with her dark and freckled hand.

8

One day you wake up, the mountains are all there,
accounted for, but cardboard, simply cut like a backdrop
in a play and slid behind the modest foreground hills,
less functional than decoys, made as much from granite
and schist, from the hot upheavals of this earth as say
wallpaper. These mountains were invented for the sake of art,
a sort of decorative frieze around the western borders
of the lake, they have no shadows, no shelters, no depth,
no cairns, nothing hides there, no fox, bobcat, deer,
nothing with eyesight, nothing that hoots or wails at night,
they are less than words, less than poems, but you are
grateful. You actually feel blessed they have appeared.

9

Is it a thought if you think it and never speak it
or write it down? Of course it is, but what if it
slips through, slips by, you know the way a thought,
I'm not talking about inconsequential stuff, I mean
something of significance you could use, make a
story from, but it gets away, dives down like a
loon who's been gliding in the periphery of your
sight and you wanted to see it, almost did, in fact
did for a second, but it was too quick to really
give it form, and you lean toward it, maybe gesture

with your arm, hoping it will return, but what if
it doesn't, what if it's really gone, does it exist
somewhere, is someone climbing it like a peak,
does he look back toward your deck chair and see
nothing?

10

He scans the telescope across the sky and finds
a galaxy: Sombrero in Virgo. Look, he says. You
put your eye to the eyepiece, peer into the distant
past, try to relax. Avert your vision, he tells
you, the galaxy is dim, a blur, it comes and goes,
focus on a nearby star. Maybe you see it, it might
be drifting by, a galaxy shaped like a hat, a thought
he planted in your mind shaped like a galaxy, a wildly
spinning hat whose light has traveled thirty million
light years to this lens, to your iris which isn't
sure what it's seeing any more. You *say* you see it,
maybe you *do, you want* to see it. You want this galaxy
to be as clear as a jewel you can wear, like Saturn.
You breathe, try to open other apertures besides
your eyes, the synapse of your brain, you dream
the galaxy, it slides like dust specks on the insides
of your lids, like some old passion you can only sense.

11

What if you came to the lake for two weeks and the mountains
never appeared. You'd never been here before. You aren't
a person into maps. Anyway, what of maps! All winter,
you'd remember the loons and Buck Island's trees silvered
by the mist, and the sharp sweet scent of the forest floor.
A family from Hartford takes the cottage after you.
The weather clears. The children can name every peak.
One day they take a picnic to Pequaket. Make no mistake,
they see everything, everything in two states, hawks
gliding by, they fill their bags with dark ripe berries,
they eat, they point to the spot on a distant beach
where only this morning they lay on their raft. In January,
they hold this day like a candle warming the winter
solstice, naming the mountains into life.

12

Paddle into the center of the lake at midnight. The sky is black.
The shoreline is black. The virgin pines are black. The mountains
are all black. None of this is true. There are seven lights from
cottages and a billion stars. Mars makes a red spot on the water.
Everything is with us now, the stars, impossible during the day,
etch their way across the universe. We feel the earth turn. The
water, the lake shore, the mountains, every boulder and tree turn
with us. Every memory is with us, the dead and the living we have
loved, our grown children as infants, past dogs and birds, arguments
and passion, certain bouquets and scents of apple groves, every
thought that's left the mind. Events that happened. And did not.
And have yet to happen. You can hold them or let them go or simply
pass your hand, your voice right through. Tonight, there are no
mountains on this lake. Yet they turn with us, purple, green, gauze,
or gray. Possibly we *are* here, black flat shapes in a black canoe,
turning swiftly through indifferent space.

SEVEN

Too many things dying and growing up.

THESE DAYS

too many things dying and growing up. Husbands
don't stick it out like they used to, and daughters
can't be counted on to stay children. Too many
things needing repair, old piano getting too dry
to make music up here in this air, and my dad
needs a new start on his worn out heart, even my
wonderful thighs getting sort of bluey and thin,
and a real web of wrinkles under my eyes, can't
keep up, can't win. Too much flowering and going by.
It's quicker than I ever thought, this growing up,
this moving out. No one going to hold back or wait
till I'm ready, not even me, not even these rose
petals dropping down like loose skin, not even
you, daddy, who begins life again, and especially
not you my children who are dying to bloom and
fruit, to consume and be consumed. Quick!
I better love you up before the next full moon
comes tugging at us, making us into something new,
who knows what.

A LIVING ANYTIME

My tailor, Mr. Rozenberg, who tells me not to make my
skirts so short, (he looks after my interests), says he has
seventy-three million dollars saved up, one for every year
of his life, that's why he only charges four dollars a hem.
He has his health, I guess he means, which is like being rich,
or at least that was my grandpa's line. Or maybe Mr.
Rozenberg really does have seventy-three million dollars
stashed away in coat hems and secret pockets and just works
sixty hours a week because he's so deft with pins and still
gets a kick from looking at people's knees. And Ida, his
wife, hasn't taken a day off since her daughter, Judith (same
name as mine) gave birth eight years ago, because, what
would she do at home? play bridge? He's like an oil mag-
nate, who ever heard of a water magnate, he says sitting on
the floor deciding how much of my ankle will show. It'll
just keep gushing out until he hits a hundred. What do you
do with your millions, I ask the three of him in the three-way
mirror. Nothing, he says. My wife takes care of it. He
winks. She winks. All of us and our many faces in the
three-way mirror wink too. Be happy, says Mr. Rozenberg
dashing soap marks all around the wool. You can make
a living anytime.

HAPPY ANIVERSARY SAYS MY EX-HUSBAND OVER THE PHONE

a safe distance away, it would have been our
fifteenth he says and I search through my mind for
today's date to see what I have missed celebrating
since I am a person who will celebrate anything
in order to dance a little or get flowers, but I have
forgotten this one, an event worth celebrating
in itself, though I dimly remember being married,
was it three or four years ago, I try going at it
backwards and forward and can't quite pin down
the day he left though the day he left I thought
I'd never forget it. Things blur, how many years
I've lived in this house, my own age, which
husband my friends are on, whether it's loosestrife
or fireweed on the route to Maine. Some things are
certain, the names of my children, the death of my
mother, the thickness of lentil soup, the uneven
humming of my typewriter, the pleasure of words
on a page. And some things sharpen, the pain
in my breast before I bleed, the old men I remember
chanting their prayers in the sanctuary, my father's
glass factory by the putrid creek, and the taste
of a peach I ate once in the Peloponnese. What was
so important is milkweed now. What is important
today will be foam at the water's edge. Laughter
is good. Some comfort is desirable. Even if we miss
this anniversary, time clicks by like a freight train.
The children cross streets and speak of God and
sex. Grey hairs streak through the chestnut,
my stomach rounds. Congratulations, I say,
knowing I would not know these things if I'd made
it to the fifteenth. Or perhaps I would.

Kezar Lake, Once in October

Once we came in October. It was too cold, really, it was
meant to be a summer place, but the pleasures of August
were too great to be abandoned. Leaves dipped their gold tips
to the lake's edge pushing off gold medallions along the onyx
surface. On Blueberry Mountain, the sky yawned wide to all
the ranges of two adjacent states and the old apple grove
dropped its sad pungent fruit in the pasture. In the brilliant
night, we pulled on wool pants and parkas, wrapped ourselves
in quilts and paddled to the middle of the lake to see
Andromeda spin out like talc. From the stern, you bent
toward me. I was facing forward and only sensed you shift
your weight. I turned around - you rose. "Kiss me,"
you said and no wonder! All this bitter sweetness of the autumn
days, constellations we had never seen so deeply,
the uncluttered loving at middle age. You took a step,
eagerly, reaching. The Old Towne listed, slid beneath
the oily surface in slow motion like a whale. We leaned and lay
down in the black water. All this without sound. As I said,
it was night in October, no one was in the lakeside camps, we
had enough goose down to climb Mt. Everest, and it was rapidly
sucking up the lake. We left the swamped canoe, and peeled away
some layers pushing and dragging them along. Twice, you didn't
answer when I called. I couldn't see to save you and even if
I could, I had to clutch the faded quilt, head for shore, alone
at night in a Maine lake where one of us drowned, the headlines
read, in an accident no one could explain. At the rocks,
I grasped the weeping aspen. You struggled out behind.
Isn't this how so much well-intentioned loving ends.
Shivering and speechless, we lugged our soggy garments
down the waterline.

MODERN TIMES

We're one of those modern couples who maintain two
separate households and two separate families to the benefit
of the Gross National Product and an evening out means
two separate baby sitters and when we visit the nurseries,
what appears to be one couple buying in bulk is really two
individuals visualizing two very different yards, and once
we've spent all our separate hard earned income on what
seems like a few scruffy clumps of perennials, (the same
flowers, we reflect later, that grow wild along the roadsides
in Maine,) we come home, and divide the clumps, going off
to plant beds and borders and fences, alone. What joy!
kneeling in the dark earth, clawing at old roots, hurrying
to put in the drooping blooms before they wilt completely,
dusk coming on, close to each other in the pure joy of
gardening, but alone, each with a hose, watering and
admiring our own designs, hopeful the plants will return
each spring, filling out, thickening like we are at middle age,
in love with our own yards, our own work, promising
silently we will never leave, rooting ourselves along with the
coreopsis and lythrum, digging in, digging in.

PORCH LOVING

Down here laying low on the front porch, we
imagine it's private, a thin vine, a short fir, a lacy
balustrade. We are hugging it up under the sheet
and soon your friend is up as we knew all along it
would be and before I blink you're naked on the
porch, your freckles glow under the street lamp,
your cock nodding stiffly in the warm air. Hello,
hello it might be saying to the Silverman's daughter
just returning from the Cape, but it's too busy in me
now speaking to that other darkness, that other
warmth and the sheet, our excuse at decorum
is almost useless billowing and slipping off our skin.
I speculate on neighbors so respectable they barely
make love in their beds let alone down on the porch
only a wilted pansy patch from the curb. Bullshit
you say, they're all doing it in the dark recesses of
their respective porches while the old setter comes
sniffing, all of us are sniffing and licking, there are
fingers in every orifice. What's the difference, we all
speak the same language. A door slams, a car starts,
all is quiet on the street. Our low moaning from
behind the landscape gardening could be anything,
an aquarium with a faulty motor, a fog horn gone
beserk and recuperating in the city, but it's not.
I come, you come, tum de dum and I come and once
again, voices in the street ho hum just resting here
down on the floor at 44 Avon Road, a single family
residence, the authorities nod, the folks in the street
applaud, we stand and bow both naked as moths
and flicker in through the screen trailing sperm
sweet sweet.

TRINKETS OF MIDDLE AGE

The park closes at dusk. The gate at the entrance is shut,
but at the exit, the chain lies down along the road like
a flattened snake. We simply drive up the wrong way,
past the sign - No Entry, and park at the top among
the Hondas and the old Volvos of the kids who shout
from car to car, their music clotting in the April night.
Below the black lawns of Anderson Hill, below the pearly
sky, Boston spirals out all glitter and height, braids and
scatters of rhinestone. We fit the Questar into its tripod
and let the parts cool: lens, prism, tube, like a teenage
boy pulling himself together before the plunge. We stare
into darkness so our eyes adjust. Nothing is sudden.
It takes time to peel away the skin of the universe.
Doors slam. Engines die out. Come alive. Cars depart,
arrive. Kids intersect, rearrange and from the far corner
of the asphalt lot, we see the blue pinpoint of a dashboard
light. We scan the skies and out of what seems blank
as the face of an eight ball, rise messages: yes/no/
perhaps, Castor/Pollux/Venus/ Arcturus/Polaris/
Cygnus and from the depth, a school of silver fish,
our Milky Way. Is anyone out there? Hear me. Ignore
the throbbing rock of youth. Here. The steady rhythm
of a grown-up heart. At the source of the blue light,
no human form is visible, only wisps of breath. Inside,
we imagine arms, legs, torsos, the outer layers peeled
away, a scanning of earthbound bodies, a deep probe
of inner space. We are doing *this* instead of *that*,
pointing the sleek telescope toward some new celestial
object we have not enjoyed before. So this is middle age,
one eye pressed to the focal point where bent light
gathers, makes sense for a moment before it splays out,
evaporates; a passion for context, for contact beyond
coupling, for a glimpse of Saturn riding by
in its platinum rings.

VALENTINE'S DAY

We step out of the plane that delivers us from winter
and the humid Florida air wraps its arms around us like
overzealous relatives and by 2, we are on the beach, barefoot
and leaping ecstatically toward the jetty which starts solid
but dissipates into an expansive sea. Already my bones
soften, my wrinkles smooth out a bit, my mind rigid with
January ice stops fending things off and my son who is
eleven says thank you for bringing us here, thank you
for taking us to beautiful places, for bringing us to see
Grandpa and Florence, thank you for this bathing suit
and this shell, for caring about nature and teaching us
to care, for writing poems and making me proud of you,
for loving your work and for loving us; he is chanting
in the rhythm of our walking, sinking in a bit with each step
and glancing over at me to see the effect, as if he were
casting for my heart and knew exactly where it lurked,
so I smile, I am cautious and say thank you for thanking me,
and my son says thank you for being Jewish and thank you
for not being too Jewish, and for being a Democrat
and believing what I believe, and for helping your friends
when they need it. Our hands bump and grip, he is grinning
because he knows he has got the perfect line, the exact fly
for this fish, we both know it and leap over the blue balloons
of Portuguese-men-of war, fallen domes of the sky,
and thank you, my son says, for knowing jellyfish and stars,
relativity and the names of quarks, we are swinging our
hands wildly, flying now towards the jetty which comes
too quickly towards us, which stops the motion of sand
and waves, and thank you for being my mother and marry-
ing dad and getting divorced so I can see each of you alone,
and thank you for picking me when you couldn't have
your own, he says. Thank you for picking *me* when you
couldn't have *your* own, I say, as he reels in my heart, that
fat red catch which for all its battles and scars heals instantly
as it soars out of my chest through the tropic sky.

EXAMPLE

We used to be obsessed with the loons' wildness,
their piercing cry and the way they dove into
another time zone and disappeared, also their
powerful bodies and white markings on sleek backs,
gorgeous neckbands, and beaks like black swords.
Not now. It's something else, closer to us.
But simpler. Domestic. Mom, dad, and chick
gliding around the peaceful lake, nuzzling,
encouraging the little one to fish; now that it's
getting to be late summer, even flight lessons
starting, dad demonstrating that crazy rowing
of the wings to move down the long runway they need
to lift off; baby doesn't even try yet, just pays
attention by his mother's side, wheezing his immature
call, like a child with asthma who just ran home,
you can hear it halfway across the lake wondering
what in god's name could make a sound like that!
How surprised the chick must be when its song
transforms, pours out sharp and hot as fire.
Dad distracting you for hours calling and
splashing, diving and playing games, while mom
and chick slip home. Love, protect, eat, mind
your own business, prepare to let go. Simple.
Why can't we? Sing when there's danger, or when
the lake is gold and black with evening light,
for the sheer joy.

Judith W. Steinbergh

Judith W. Steinbergh was born in 1943, grew up in western Pennsylvania, and graduated from Wellesley College in 1965. She has published *Marshmallow Worlds* (Grosset & Dunlap, 1972), *Lillian Bloom, A Separation* (Wampeter Press, 1980), and *Motherwriter* (Wampeter Press, 1983). She co-authored with Elizabeth McKim, *Beyond Words, Writing Poems with Children,*(Wampeter Press, 1983.) Judith has worked for sixteen years as Poet-in-the Schools throughout Massachusetts and is currently Writer-in-Residence in the Brookline Public Schools. She has taught at Tufts University and at Lesley College in Cambridge, MA. She has lectured and given readings at many colleges and universities on the east coast. Judith also performs original songs and poems with Victor Cockburn of Troubadour and has collaborated on three tapes for children and one tape for adults (Feel Yourself in Motion, 1986.) She lives with her two children in Brookline, MA.